THE ULTIMATE HOT AIR BALLOON BUCKET LIST

100 Ballooning Things to Do Before You Die

by Barbe Awalt

Río Grande Books
Los Ranchos, NM

The Bucket List Book Series

The Basic New Mexico Bucket List by Barbe Awalt

The Ultimate Hot Air Balloon Bucket List by Barbe Awalt

The Complete Cowboy Bucket List by Slim Randles (2015)

The Complete Shopping Bucket List by Barbe Awalt (2016)

The Complete Space Buff's Bucket List by Loretta Hall (2016)

Copyright © 2015 Barbe Awalt

Published by Río Grande Books
925 Salamanca NW, Los Ranchos, NM 87107-5647
505-344-9382   www.LPDPress.com

Printed in the United States of America
Book Design: Paul Rhetts

Library of Congress Cataloging-in-Publication Data

Awalt, Barbe.
 The complete hot air balloon bucket list : 100 ballooning things to do
before you die / by Barbe Awalt.
    pages cm. -- (The bucket list book series)
 Includes webography.
 ISBN 978-1-936744-34-3 (paperback : alk. paper)
1. Ballooning--Miscellanea. I. Title.
 GV762.A93 2015
 797.5'1--dc23
                                    2015018621

Albuquerque International Balloon Fiesta®, Twilight Twinkle Glow™,
Balloon Glow™, and Night Magic Glow™ are registered trademarks.

*Front cover: Sun Flyer and After Midnight balloons. Courtesy of Paul
Rhetts. Back cover: Balloons over the Fiesta field (courtesy of Barbe Awalt)
and Dawn Patrol (courtesy of Kim Vesely).*

CONTENTS

Stormy day along Concession Row at Albuquerque International Balloon Fiesta. Courtesy of Barbe Awalt

The Zia and Colorado High balloons at Snowmass, Colorado. Courtesy of Mary McConnell

The Hot Air Balloon Bucket List

If you live in Albuquerque, you are involved in ballooning. Albuquerque is "The Hot Air Ballooning Capital of the World." Hot air ballooning is the biggest show on earth or in the sky. You can fly, you can chase, you can be a spectator, or you can be involved with the many events and businesses associated with ballooning. Where else can you see a beautiful rainbow of balloons on the way to work?

The Albuquerque International Balloon Fiesta® takes place every October—the first two full weekends, the week between, and the days before. The opening school/community event is Albuquerque Aloft and it is a chance for students to see balloons, pilots, and crew up close. Hot air balloons are the Official Transportation Vehicle of New Mexico.

The locals in Albuquerque love to belittle the Balloon Fiesta—the traffic, the crowds, the events—did I mention the traffic? Balloon Fiesta brings major money into Albuquerque every year. After they see the balloons in the air, the locals melt. I am sure there are other places that have a "box" but the Albuquerque Box is famous.

This book was written to honor ballooning, the many people past and present who have made ballooning fun, to help newbies learn about ballooning, and to mark the 10th Anniversary of the Anderson–Abruzzo Albuquerque International Balloon Museum. I have had unprecedented access to ballooning over many years and this is my Hot Air Balloon Bucket List.

I wish to thank: Paul Rhetts, Frank Bacon, Bill & Barbara Douglas, Mary & Tom McConnell, Dick Brown, Kim Vesely, Ana & Josh Bacon, Troy & Tami Bradley, Steve Stucker & KOB, John T. Denne, Ron Behrmann, James Blackburn, the *Albuquerque Journal*, Tania Goldfeder, Royal Balloon-Cappadocia/Turkey and Suat Ulusoy, Mukul Tamsekar, Lisa Mulder, RE/MAX and Kristen McCloy, Ivan Trifonov, Lois Mayland, Loretta Hall, Pam Micker, Kim Jew Photography, Kristy Hannun Baker, Ken Tuley (Top Gun), Diane Karlsson & Plano Pin Company, The Anderson-Abruzzo Albuquerque International Balloon Museum, Jill Lane and The Anderson-Abruzzo Albuquerque International Balloon Museum Foundation, and the Albuquerque International Balloon Fiesta®. Thanks too to all the pilots who checked the book. In many ways, Peggy Bacon is the reason any of this has happened.

Some of the items on my list are a bit unusual but always fun and there are suggestions for wanna-be balloonists. You may have other things to add and I suggest you start your own Bucket List. There is no order except I do think you have to take a ride in a balloon first. The Anderson-Abruzzo Albuquerque International Balloon Museum and the Albuquerque International Balloon Fiesta are numbers 1 and 2 because they are most important to ballooning —at least in my Albuquerque eyes.

Information on the Anderson-Abruzzo Albuquerque International Balloon Museum Foundation is in the back of the book.

Because this is a hi-tech kind of world, many of the

entries have a website or a few afterwards. An all call went out on Facebook and there is a page at the end of Near Misses—of other ballooning things to do. Research what you are interested in. Many of the websites have contacts to get more information.

Make your own hot air balloon bucket list—use this for a guide to do your own! And above all, HAVE FUN!

Archbishop Michael J. Sheehan's first balloon ride. Courtesy of Barbe Awalt

Kellogg's and Space Shuttle balloons. Courtesy of Barbe Awalt

The List

100. Take a Balloon Ride

You don't know if you will like ballooning until you go up. It is gently floating in the air. A ride can run nothing for a freebie or hundreds of dollars. The rider's job is to look for other balloons and let the pilot know. The rider also needs to spot high voltage and electrical wires—nasty! The landing may be rough or a gentle touchdown. Do not jump out of the balloon the minute it lands. Your weight will help stabilize the balloon. Make sure you take a camera. It is a ride of a lifetime. Remember, it is a sport and with dangers. Landing in cactus or barbed wire does bring a few problems.— www.visitalbuquerque.org/things-to-do/air/ballooning/

First balloon ride for Dan Turner. Courtesy of Barbe Awalt

99. Join a Chase Crew

Chase Crews are necessary to pick up the balloon-ists wherever they land. The crew is a support gang to also inflate the balloon. The Chase Crew puts the balloon away and if necessary they supply anything the pilot needs in the way of help. They cruise around in pick-up trucks. If they are lucky they all go out for a good breakfast after ballooning. The crew is loyal to their pilot, the balloon, and each other. It is usually early morning work. Wear gloves and tennis shoes. Remember the pilot is ALWAYS in charge. Never smoke, respect the balloon, and don't step on the balloon. Respect the time when the chase truck leaves the Fiesta Field—we have left people! Each year, the Albuquerque International Balloon Fiesta® advertizes that they need crew to help with out-of-town balloons. You haven't lived until you drive a chase vehicle and have five back seat drivers!—www.coloradoballoonclub.net/chase-crewpage.html, www.balloonfiesta.com

Sun Flyer crew. Courtesy of Barbe Awalt

98. Buy a Pick-Up Truck & Maybe a Trailer

If you want to cart around a gondola, an inflator fan, balloon envelope, ropes, chase crew, and all the ballooning stuff—you need a truck. Trucks and trailers are a great place to shelter from the weather. Be aware that balloons are ripped off every year but the ones we have seen stolen recently, are in a trailer. Maybe a thief can't see what is in the trailer and is hoping for more. A trailer does keep the rain and snow from the balloon and that is important if you don't want your balloon smelling like a rotten egg. Seriously! Hot air balloons are hard to fence! Who buys a hot, hot air balloon?

SUV with balloon. Courtesy of John T. Denne

97. Collect & Trade Balloon Pins & Patches

Start trading pins with your crew then progress to other balloon crews. You need to start with a "stash" so either purchase pins from your pilot or get a bunch on eBay or a store. The big balloon pin company is Plano Pins in Texas. The last few years they have made people crazy with their Breaking Bad balloon pins. You can also get pins and patches from the Anderson-Abruzzo Albuquerque International Balloon Museum Shoppe and various balloon stores. The Albuquerque International Balloon Fiesta® and Anderson-Abruzzo Albuquerque International Balloon Museum both hold ballooning trading events.—www.planopin.com, www.pinlady.com

Breaking Bad pin. Courtesy of Plano Pin Company and Diane Karlsson

96. See Steve Stucker be Memorable

Albuquerque KOB TV Weatherman, Steve Stucker, is known for his balloon pin coat and very large (and heavy!) balloon hat. He is famous and has broadcasted, on KOB TV in his outfit, for 25 years. Steve is locally colorful. Steve also knows everyone in ballooning and is a wealth of information. Rain, snow, cold, or wind, Steve is on the Fiesta Field doing his thing. Thanks Steve! You are loved and an institution!—www.kob.com/article/stories/s53790.shtml#.VO9gOOCe3fg

Steve Stucker. Courtesy KOB 4/Kim Jew Photography

95. Read the Official *Albuquerque Journal* Supplement

The supplement insert comes out right before Balloon Fiesta from the *Albuquerque Journal*. It has human-interest stories, events, the entire schedule of Balloon Fiesta, and listings of the balloons and pilots. It also tells you what is new this year at Fiesta. It is a bargain and a must have!—www.abqjournal.com

Balloon Fiesta Supplement. Copyright: Albuquerque Journal. Reprinted with permission

94. Get Christened

After your first balloon ride you get christened. It is supposed to be with champagne but frankly we have done it with soda and water. Champagne means planning ahead and sometimes we are not real good with that! The pilot recites the *Balloonist's Prayer* (Irish Blessing) and then you drink from a cup while kneeling. Your "sponsor" then gently or roughly, rubs dirt in your hair. Then everyone kisses and hugs you. Nice. We will admit going out to eat with mud in your hair can be interesting.

Balloonist's Prayer
May the winds welcome you with softness,
May the sun bless you with its warm hands,
May you fly so high and so well that God
joins you in laughter and sets you gently
back into the loving arms of Mother Earth.

First flight christening. Courtesy of Barbe Awalt

93. Read the Official Balloon Fiesta Program

The Albuquerque International Balloon Fiesta® Program is a collector's item. It is thick, it is glossy, has a lot of information, and articles on ballooning things you have to know. You can get it at the Albuquerque International Balloon Fiesta Store at the headquarters or on the Fiesta Field. It also has a map of the Fiesta field and that is handy!—www.balloonfiesta.com

Albuquerque International Balloon Fiesta Program.

92. Read Balloon Books

There is no better way to learn about ballooning, the history, and the people who made it special. These are some of our favorites but there are many more:

The World Comes To Albuquerque—by Dick Brown, Kim Vesely, Dr. Tom McConnell, and Paul Rhetts (out of print, but you still may be able to find it), the best balloon book to commemorate the 40th anniversary of ballooning in Albuquerque.

Balloon Safety Seminars—by Dr. Tom McConnell, very technical but if you fly you need to read this.

Aloft—by Douglas Heller & Bobbi Valentine, a great photo souvenir of Balloon Fiesta

Balloons Over Albuquerque—by Steve Larese

Balloon Flying Handbook—by The Federal Aviation Administration (Available on eBay)

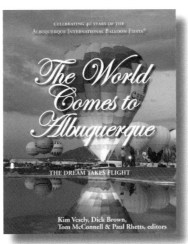

Official book of the 40th Balloon Fiesta. Courtesy of Rio Grande Books, publisher.

91. Be a Top Gun

The Top Gun Ballooning Club is New Mexico's premiere club for competition hot air ballooning pilots. It is also a cool thing to get involved with if you just want to observe. They have monthly competitive events. Top Gun is affiliated with the Balloon Federation of America through the Hot Air Competitive Division.—www. topgunballooning.org

Top Gun Logo. Courtesy of Ken Tuley

90. Gift a Kid's Book on Ballooning

There is nothing better than reading to a kid and they want to know your ballooning stories. Books make great souvenirs or a treasured gift. Try these for a child in your life and there are many more:

Meet Me At The Balloon Museum—by Travelin' Jack

Pop Flop—by Nancy Abruzzo

Hot Foot Teddy—by Sue Houser

Paloma & the Dust Devil at the Balloon Festival—by Marcy Heller

Stasha Dog's Secret Dream: A Hot Air Balloon Adventure—by Tomi Jill Folk

The Elephants in the Land of Enchantment—by Beverly Eschberger

Curious George and the Hot Air Balloon—by H.A. Rey & Margret Rey

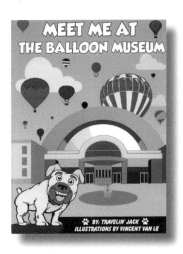

Meet Me at the Balloon Museum *by Travelin' Jack, Enchantment Lane Publications, publisher.*

89. Visit a Balloon Event in Another Part of the U.S.A. or World

There are rallies, balloon events, parades, and glows all over the world. Balloonists need to get together to fly and party. Make sure you catch the Preakness Turf Valley Ballooning event, Lift Off Levin, Taos Mountain Balloon Rally, Elephant Butte Balloon Regata, the Great Reno Balloon Race, The Great Texas Balloon Race, Lorraine Mondial, Yunnan Hot Air Balloon Carnival, Vernon Winter Carnival Hot Air Balloon Fiesta & Glow, and the Atlantic International Balloon Fiesta among many more.—www.hotairballoon.com

Most Wonderful. Courtesy of John T. Denne

88. Buy Balloon Themed Clothes or a Costume

Who knows when you will need a ballooning vest, sweater, tie, or even a tablecoth? See it is a problem —where to stop? Of course you can visit many ballooning or regular stores. Or be very crafty and make something yourself. There is an assortment of hot air balloon fabric. Try Southwest Decoratives in Albuquerque near Fiesta Field for knowledgeable people and a good selection of patterns: www.swdecoratives.com. Your crew can also wear matching outfits that complement your balloon from simple to complicated.

Balloon costume. Courtey of John T. Denne

87. Join Quad A (AAAA)

Or it is officially, the Albuquerque Aerostat Ascension Association. It is the largest community ballooning organization in the world. They have many educational seminars and a chance to meet the ballooning pilots and fanatics. It is the place to hear about events and meet people you would like to learn more from. They sponsor on Valentine's Weekend, the Friends & Lovers Rally now at Balloon Fiesta Field in Albuquerque (formerly in Rio Rancho).—www.hotairballooning.org

**Albuquerque Aerostat
Ascension Association**
Albuquerque, New Mexico

Logo. Courtesy of AAAA

86. Visit Other Balloon Museums

There are many hot air balloon museums in the world and some are listed. Be aware that many science museums also have dedicated space to the magic of lighter than air.

National Balloon Museum, Indianola, Iowa: www.nationalballoonmuseum.com

British Balloon Museum & Library, Old Windsor, England: www.bbml.org.uk

Balloon Preservation Group, Sussex, England

Airship Plaza, Lelystad, Netherlands

Château de Balleroy, Balleroy, France—A Malcolm Forbes Museum in a castle to host his collection. It is considered the first international ballooning museum, started in 1975. www.chateau-balleroy.fr

Zeppelin Museum, Friedrichshafen, Germany—The Museum opened in 1996 and has a scale reproduction of the Hindenburg. www.zepplin-museum.de

Logo. Courtesy of the National Balloon Museum

85. Take Balloon Pictures

When there was film, The Albuquerque International Balloon Fiesta® was the most photographed event in the world. You could measure how many rolls were developed. Now with digital photography it is probably even more popular because you can just shoot away. Get a camera, visit balloons, and start snapping pictures. If you ride, the view is incredible and you will want to remember it. Share your pictures and even enter them in contests.

Balloons. Courtesy of John T. Denne

84. If You Don't Know about Breakfast Burritos - Learn

Sure you can get hot chocolate, fried potatoes, beer, donuts, but you need a burrito! Go along Concession Row at the Balloon Fiesta and there are all kinds of burritos. Ballooning is known for burritos—at least in New Mexico. You can buy a burrito frozen or in a store but why?

Burrito. Courtesy of Paul Rhetts

83. Who Is "Professor" P.A. Van Tassell?

He is the Albuquerque bartender who piloted on July 4, 1882, a "gas bag" from Second Street in Albuquerque, up 14,000 feet. He is the first documented New Mexican to fly a balloon. The balloon was made from cattle intestines and cost $850. It came from California. It was christened the City of Albuquerque and needed 30,000 cubic feet of coal gas to inflate. Van Tassel later flew in LA, San Francisco, Siam, India, Australia, Hawaii, and finally Bengal, where his wife died in a balloon fall. Later he owned the Captain P.A. Van Tassel Toy Balloon Mfg. Co.

Inflation of Van Tassel's balloon on Second Street, between Railroad (now Central Ave) and Gold streets in 1882, at the site of the present-day Sunshine Building. Courtesy of the William F. Stamm family and Dick Brown

82. View Balloon Films

There have been many great hot air balloon films. But the best may be the oldies.

The Wizard of Oz—1931
Around the World in 80 Days—1956
The Great Race—1965
Up—2009

Remember to view the recent videos made of the Albuquerque International Balloon Fiesta or ballooning in general. Get them at the Anderson-Abruzzo Albuquerque International Balloon Museum Shoppe, the AIBF® store or on eBay. Check out the RE/MAX balloon on TV ads to put you in the mood to fly.

RE/MAX Balloon. Courtesy of Kristen McCloy

81. Learn the Differences between Hot Air & Gas Balloons

The America's Challenge™ takes place every year at the Balloon Fiesta. The object is to fly the greatest distance from Albuquerque. The America's Challenge was founded by the Balloon Fiesta in 1995 largely due to the efforts and vision of Mark Sullivan. The race is modeled after the Gordon Bennett Cup but America's Challenge is open to all countries and there is no limit of entries per country. Gas ballooning is helium and hydrogen while regular hot air ballooning is propane based. The gas balloons are up for days and both kinds of balloons launch from the balloon field. Troy Bradley of Albuquerque and Leonid Tiukhtyaev of Russia now own the gas balloon record. The Two Eagles Balloon launched in January 2015, from Saga, Japan, and landed in Mexico. www.npr.org

The Gordon Bennett Gas Balloon Race comes to Albuquerque during Fiesta when an American team wins it the year before.

Gas balloons. Courtesy of Tom McConnell

80. Take a Mass Ascension Ride

The ultimate balloon experience is a balloon ride from the field during the Mass Ascension at Albuquerque International Balloon Fiesta®. Watch out for the christening afterwards! Make sure to get a balloon pin and card from YOUR balloon pilot. After your ride, you need to go the Anderson-Abruzzo Albuquerque International Balloon Museum in Albuquerque to study and buy stuff. It is said, your first balloon ride is free and the next is $50,000—for a new balloon. We hope you get an Albuquerque Box!—www.balloonfiesta.com, www.hotairballooning.com, www.balloonmuseum.com

Mass Ascension. Courtesy of Barbe Awalt

79. Build a Tie Dye Balloon

Jonathan Wolfe is the lead designer, artist, and pilot of Skydyes! He burst on the balloon scene in 2001 with his first tie-dye balloon, Gloria Caeli, Glory of the Sky. She was a Piccard inspired pattern with 168 connected panels, 10000 meters of fabric, and took 6 months to dye and build. The basket was even woven using a custom design inspired by the work of Bert Padelt. His new venture is computer generated decorated hot air balloons. They are called Flying Fractal Art Balloons. Jonathan lives and works in Albuquerque and has a Ph.D. in neuroscience. He made his first prototype in Vermont where he took his first balloon ride and learned how to make balloons. "If you want it enough you can build your own flying machine."—http://skydyes.com

Gloria Caeli balloon. Courtesy of Tania Goldfeder

78. Read about the Titans of Ballooning

Without the giants of ballooning history, we would not know or enjoy the sport like we do.

Sid Cutter was the founder of Balloon Fiesta. He threw a party, bought a balloon for it, and taught himself to fly. He held many records and awards for his flying. Tom Rutherford, manager of KOB-FM radio, is the voice of Fiesta. He was vice-president of World Balloon Corporation and a noted pilot. Ben Abruzzo was one of the original 13 pilots for the first Balloon Fiesta at Coronado Center. Ben and Maxie Anderson attempted the first Atlantic crossing in the *Double Eagle I Balloon*. Richard Abruzzo, Ben's son, disappeared with Carol Rymer Davis over the Adriatic Sea while competing in the 2010 Gordon Bennett Cup. Maxie Anderson made the first Trans-North American non-stop balloon trip. He was also killed in the Gordon Bennett Cup. Troy Bradley, on the board of the Anderson-Abruzzo Balloon Museum Foundation, just recently set a gas ballooning record in the *Two Eagles* balloon. Mark Sullivan holds numerous records as well. There are so many more.

Anderson-Abruzzo Albuquerque International Balloon Museum bumper sticker

77. Do a Splash 'n Dash

A Splash 'n Dash is any body of water that is targeted by a pilot to drop in and then fly out. The aim is to get passengers' feet wet. It is tricky because if you go too deep in the water you can get stuck in mud. The Splash 'n Dash is famous at Fiesta because balloons love to drop into the Rio Grande. The City of Albuquerque river crafts occasionally get called out for a stranded balloon in the river.

Splash 'n Dash in the Rio Grande. Courtesy of Ron Behrmann

76. Volunteer

There are so many opportunities to volunteer and enjoy the balloons at the same time. Balloon Fiesta has almost 1,000 volunteers (called "Navigators;" www.balloonfiesta.com/operations/volunteering). Crewing for a balloon may build long friendships. Even the parking, the sale of programs on the field, and vendors' tents use volunteers at Balloon Fiesta. The Anderson-Abruzzo Albuquerque International Balloon Museum has volunteers year-round. Any museum that features balloons needs and uses volunteers.

Balloons at Balloon Fiesta. Courtesy of Barbe Awalt

75. Donate Your Balloon Memorabilia

Sometimes when cleaning out the treasures you have boxed away, you find ballooning memorabilia. Collectors have put away programs, pins, patches, cards, photos, video, and jackets that museums would love to display. Sometimes even old balloon envelopes and baskets are donated. Remember you can't take it with you! Make sure others can enjoy and learn from your items. Talk to a museum curator to find out what they need. If you donate items you may be able to benefit from a tax write-off. Nice!

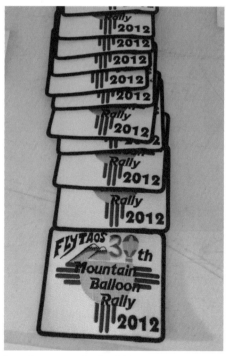

Balloon patches. Courtesy of John T. Denne

74. Enjoy Balloons & Tailgate

If you are a member of a Chase Crew you tailgate. Whether it is eating from the concessions on the Fiesta Field, picnicking, or pitching a tent and making a day of it. Spectators bring in food. Let's face it, some of the concessions are expensive and especially for a large group. The whole idea is to have fun no matter what socio-economic level you are in.

Balloons at Balloon Fiesta. Courtesy of Barbe Awalt

73. Buy a Balloon Toy

The hottest toys are kites and inflatable balloons but you can get any toys and have fun with your favorite kid. The best toys can also teach science or history. Get books, kits, posters, and things kids will love but learn from too. After you see the balloons fly, kids want to fly something. Big kids love toys too!

Discover Balloon store, Old Town Albuquerque. Courtesy of Barbe Awalt

72. Wander Concession Row at a Balloon Event

What could be better than eating and shopping? Some balloon festivals have an extensive collection of vendors. You can get every food item imaginable: burritos, sandwiches, fried stuff on a stick, BBQ, anything green chile, and donuts. Visit a beer garden. There can also be an arts and crafts tent. Many vendors can have handmade items for sale and anything balloon can be bought. There are even cars, trucks, and hot air balloon tents if you feel the urge for a big purchase. You can get free samples. Many have said it is like walking a boardwalk at the beach. We love the big Johnsonville sausage grill truck at Fiesta! Yum!

Concession Row at Balloon Fiesta. Courtesy of Tom McConnell and the Albuquerque International Balloon Fiesta®

71. Get a Cool Jacket

In the early days, prior to 9/11, we used to fly out of the Albuquerque airport wearing our Official Sponsor Balloon jackets. They were cool. The jackets have Sponsor patches and balloon pins. People stopped and looked and some even asked about it. There are great jackets to buy.

Assorted jackets from the Sun Flyer crew. Courtesy of Barbe Awalt

70. Take a Tethered Balloon Ride

Tethering a balloon means it is anchored by a rope usually to a pick-up truck. It is a good way to give a lot of people a ride up 150 feet and down. Balloons can also be tied down when the wind is a problem while inflating. Make sure you NEVER get wrapped up in the tie down rope. NEVER walk on a rope!

Today Show's Al Roker and his first balloon ride (albeit tethered). Courtesy of Barbe Awalt

69. Zebras

Zebras are the launch directors at balloon events. The pilot-in-command may have the final word about launching, but Zebras give permission to launch. The pilot may not launch without that permission. Zebras are the on-field safety people. They know ballooning and most are pilots. Zebras wear black and white. They look strange but they are all business. They just don't step in to do the Zebra job. They train for months in all kinds of scenarios. Pilots look for the Zebra's famous "thumbs up" to launch. They have cool pins too!

Zebra Pam Micker directing balloon traffic. Courtesy of Lois Mayland

68. Sunset Ballooning

We have the best sunsets in New Mexico and they are great elsewhere too. There is nothing better than a hot air balloon taking two people up for a romantic ride. A ride is the ultimate souvenir. Don't forget a camera! The best place to see sunset ballooning is on the Sandias. You can look out at the sunset and any balloons flying. You can even have a margarita!

Contrails over balloons. Courtesy of John T. Denne

67. See the Flight of the Nations

Flight of the Nations is held every Wednesday of Albuquerque International Balloon Fiesta® and it is a Mass Ascension to honor all the counties at that year's Fiesta. Up to two balloons from every country launch after the event Sponsor Balloon launches. Each balloon carries their country's flag.—www.balloonfiesta.com

Mass Ascension. Courtesy of Barbe Awalt

66. Use GoPros

GoPro® cameras are one of the new things to visit balloons. Mount the GoPro® camera on the gondola and film the entire trip. Combine with music and post it. See what has been done on YouTube and Facebook.—http://gopro.com

Courtesy of GoPro®

65. Photograph Balloons Professionally

Professional photographers usually take millions of photos of balloons and sell them to magazines, publishers, television, calendars, and websites. They capture truly beautiful and remarkable moments on film or as digital images.

Koshare Balloon at Taos Balloon Rally. Courtesy of John T. Denne

64. Subscribe to a Balloon Magazine

The website for Blastvalve gives all kinds of contact information for balloonists.—www.Blastvalve.com

Ballooning is bi-monthly and free to members of Balloon Federation of America.—www.bfa.net

Read about festivals and the newest innovations.

Inflating Sun Flyer. Courtesy of Barbe Awalt

63. Experience the Albuquerque Box

The Albuquerque Box is a weather phenomenon. You can't steer a balloon so you rely on different winds at different altitudes. You can catch different winds by going up or down using your burner to make a box and come back where you took off. The ultimate is to land in the bed of your pick-up truck at the landing site but we aren't recommending that. The Box doesn't happen all the time but when it does you will see balloons hanging around the field for a long time.—http://theweatherprediction.com/weatherpapers/107/index.html

Balloon launch. Courtesy of Barbe Awalt

62. Take Someone to *Stories in the Sky*

Children have to read and be read to. The Anderson-Abruzzo Albuquerque International Balloon Museum has *Stories in The Sky* and *Stories in the Night Sky*. Another good place to go is Science in the Sky at the Balloon Museum. Children and adults can learn about all sorts of topics. The Museum even has a Spring Break Family Day. Stories In the Sky was voted best story time by readers of *Albuquerque The Magazine*.—www.cabq.gov/culturalservices/balloonmuseum/education-volunteering/stories-in-the-sky

Anderson-Abruzzo Albuquerque International Balloon Museum exhibit. Courtesy of Holly Lowe

61. Learn Ballooning History

The first hot air balloon was invented by Joseph Michel Montgolfier and his brother Jacques Éitenne of Annonay, France. It was 1783. Contemporary hot air ballooning began in 1960, with Ed Yost inventing and launching a new nylon envelope and propane burner. The first balloon had no basket, just a seat for Yost. In 2012, more than 2,300 balloons were registered with the FAA and another 495 commercial balloons. Arizona space tourism company, World View Enterprises broke the world record for a parafoil in 2014. Google executive, Alan Eustace broke Felix Baumgartner's record, jumping 135, 890 feet in 2014. They both jumped in Roswell, New Mexico. The sky is the limit.—www.gizmag.com/alan-eustace-world-record -skydive-stra-tex/34423/

Joseph Michel and Jaques Étienne Montgolfier

60. Pull a Rip Cord

You know the red cord to the balloon that pulls out the top? The hole lets out the hot air and allows the balloon to land. Usually the pilot pulls the cord but if you are nice to the pilot they may allow you to pull. Pulling does take elbow grease. Do not pull it by accident!

Letting the hot air out. Courtesy of Barbe Awalt

59. Fly a Hot Air Balloon or Sky Lantern

These flyable balloons are very popular in Japan, Thailand, Brazil, Mexico, and China. They are called Kongming Lanterns. They have been made for centuries. The design is a thin, paper shell with an opening at the bottom. There is a candle below the opening. They can start fires when they land. Lantern Festivals have thousands of the candles light up the night sky and you can write wishes on the balloon. You can buy a 14 pack of lantern balloons on Amazon.—www.wikipedia.org/wiki.Sky_latern

Lighting Floating Red Lantern. Courtesy of Peter Griffin

58. What Is Your Favorite Special Shape?

Some with say the balloons from Brazil are the favorites. Malcolm Forbes has some grand shapes especially with his castle. The Bee Family is a crowd pleaser along with Darth Vader, the Ristra, the Butterfly, the Stork, Angry Bird, and the Stagecoach. The old Smokey Bear Balloon got caught in a radio tower in front of our eyes. No one was hurt and there is a new Smokey Balloon to wow the crowd and prevent forest fires. Special Shapes are more expensive to build and much harder to inflate and land. The Chic-I-Boom balloon was Albuquerque's first special shape balloon, piloted by Jacques Soukup and Kirk Thomas. The balloon lives on as the name of the Anderson-Abruzzo Balloon Museum Gala.—www.druidkirk.org/balloons/index-html

Airabelle, the Creamland Cow Balloon. Courtesy of Barbe Awalt

57. Go to Rodeo & Glowdeo

Think of an event where the whole ascension is special shape balloons from all over the world. That is the Special Shape Rodeo™ and its counterpart at night the Special Shape Glowdeo™. —www.balloonfiesta.com

Special Shape Balloons at 2006 Balloon Fiesta. Courtesy of Tom McConnell

56. Salute the Flag

Before every Balloon Fiesta Mass Ascension, one or more balloons carry the American Flag. The National Anthem is sung. Some people don't know to stop everything, take off your hats, and salute the flag. Period. End of discussion. —www.balloonfiesta.com

Saluting the flag. Courtesy of Barbe Awalt

55. See Cappadocia by Balloon

Cappadocia, Turkey, is famous for their rock formations and deep valleys. Royal Balloon-Cappadocia/Turkey is a certified and unusual way to see the area and have a memorable experience. They have flown: Martha Stewart, actresses Ellen Burstyn and Eva LaRue, the Royal Queen and Princess of Bhutan, among many more.—www.royalballoon.com

Royal Balloons over tent rocks in Cappadocia, Turkey. Courtesy of Royal Balloon-Cappadocia/Turkey

54. You Need Balloon Stuff!

Who doesn't need a hot air balloon decanter? You have to have hot air balloon earrings, vests, hats, or kites. Luckily there are a lot of places that will cater to your balloon needs.

Discover Balloon 205 C San Felipe NW, Old Town, Albuquerque—www.discoverballoons.com

National Balloon Museum Store, 1601 Hwy. 65/69, Indianola, IA—www.nationalballoonmuseum.com

In the Air—www.hotairear.com

Full A Hot Air—www.fullahotair.com

Anderson-Abruzzo Albuquerque International Balloon Museum Shoppe, 9201 Balloon Museum Dr. NE—www.balloonmuseum.com

Albuquerque International Balloon Fiesta® Store, 4401 Alameda Blvd. NW—www.balloonfiestastuff.com

Balloon apparel. Courtesy of Anderson-Abruzzo Albuquerque International Balloon Museum Shoppe

53. Take the Test!

You do know just anyone can't step into a hot air balloon gondola and fly? You need a license! The minimum age to learn as a student pilot is 14. You must be able to read, write, speak, and understand English. Medically you have to be able to fly. To become a private pilot the age is 16. You do have to take a written FAA test as well as log hours, take an oral test, and do a solo flight. The FAA also requires one to pass a practical flight test administered by an examiner designated by the FAA. You can get a prep oral exam on Amazon at: www.amazon.com/Balloon-Pilot-Ultimate-Checkride-Oral/dp/B0081YBVC6, www.fun-flying.com/become-a-pilot.html

Special shape balloons at Balloon Fiesta. Courtesy of Barbe Awalt

52. Experience Stratobowl

Stratobowl is a natural environment and park in the Black Hills National Forest in South Dakota. In 1934 and 1935 the National Geographic Society and the U.S. Army launched manned balloon flights from Stratocamp. Now, in early September, a dozen experienced balloonists celebrate the early flights with a three-day rally. If everything goes well, you drop your balloon into the canyon and follow the flow to Reptile Gardens.—www.stratobowl.com

Stratobowl memorial plaque. Courtesy of Loretta Hall

51. Know the Companies

The ballooning companies have made it happen. Lindstrand, Cameron, Piccard, FireFly, UltraMagic, National Ballooning, Boland Balloons, and Raven Balloons now Aerostar Balloons, have built many hot-air balloons and are making innovations to design and technology. Gas balloons are primarily made by Wörmer in Germany. There are of course more companies and new ones every day.

Clown balloon. Courtesy of Barbe Awalt

50. There's an App for That

The cool hot air balloon game for kids is *Hot Air Balloon Survivor* by Mukul Tamsekar. It was released in 2013 for the ipad and iphone. It is free.

There are also weather apps for you iphone and ipad. http://itunes.apple.com/us/app/hot-air-balloon-survivor/id687059941?mt=8

Donkey Kong Country 2 features a balloon. *Hot Air* is a flight logging and tracking app. It is like having a log book in your pocket.

Video screen grab of Hot Air Balloon Survivor video game. Courtesy of Mukul Tamsekar

49. Do the Night Magic Glow™ & After Glow™

You have never seen anything so beautiful as balloons lighting up their burners for a glow. There is something magic and it is casual and just feels different. The sunset and glowing balloons—what could be better? And the pilots don't just switch on their burners whenever they feel like it. They have radio instructions. KKOB radio has been instrumental to give communications to pilots. After the Glow there is a great fireworks display. Get food on Concession Row, bring the family, and have fun. Did you know the first Balloon Glow was Christmas Eve 1979 for pilots to show their appreciation to the people of New Mexico?—www.balloonfiesta.com

Klondike special shape balloon at Balloon Fiesta. Courtesy of Barbe Awalt

48. Grab a Key or at Least Watch

On Friday of the Albuquerque International Balloon Fiesta® there is the famous Key Grab. It is now called the Pole Grab or Prize Grab. The feeling of a herd of balloons flying low toward poles is unbelievable! The accuracy of the pilots, the hanging out of a basket by a co-pilot trying to grab something, and the colors are inspiring. This is an AHH! Moment. —www.balloonfiesta.com

Herds of balloons at Key Grab. Courtesy of Barbe Awalt

47. Take an RV to Fiesta

The area around Fiesta Field turns into a small city. RVers can walk to the Fiesta or the Balloon Museum.—www.balloonfiesta.com

Courtesy of Anderson-Abruzzo Albuquerque International Balloon Museum

46. Go to the Great Egg Drop

The Great Egg Drop Returns! What better way to celebrate Easter than an egg drop from a hot air balloon? And of course, it happens only in Albuquerque. It has been held at Cibola High School in the Heights on the Saturday before Easter. Everyone who goes is encouraged to bring a canned food item for the Storehouse. More than 25,000 eggs were dropped! It is fun for the whole family!—www.thegreateggdrop.com

Balloon egg drop. Courtesy of Great Egg Drop

45. Do a Special "Club" during Fiesta

Sure you pay extra—Chasers Club, Gondola Club, Balloons & Breakfast, or Dine & Glow Dinner (both formerly Diamond Club)—but you get food, a seat for Mass Ascension, and parking passes—worth their weight in gold! Chasers Club and Gondola Club are right on the Fiesta Field. Balloons & Breakfast and Dine & Glow are at the Anderson-Abruzzo Albuquerque International Balloon Museum and we highly advise buying tickets early—www.balloonmuseum.com or 505/880-0500 for a group, military, or member rates.—www.balloonfiesta.com

Diamond Club. Courtesy of Anderson-Abruzzo Albuquerque International Balloon Museum

44. Name all the Balloon Fiesta Locations

1972 - Coronado Mall, Albuquerque, with 13 balloons

1973 to1974 - Albuquerque State Fair Grounds

1975 to 1980 - Simms Field, Albuquerque

1981 to 1985 - Cutter Field, Albuquerque

1986 to 1995 - Balloon Fiesta Park #1, Albuquerque

1996 to present - permanent location in North Albuquerque, Balloon Fiesta Park

Map from The World Comes To Albuquerque. *Courtesy of Rio Grande Books, publisher*

43. Know the Most Balloons in Fiesta Were...

It is reported that 1,019 balloons registered for the 2000 Fiesta (1003 balloons actually flew that year). It was a monumental Fiesta—they had moved to the new field and we had survived the great disaster that was supposed to happen with Y2K. But being there, it was dangerous. There were too many balloons and in hindsight we were all lucky that nothing happened. Balloon Fiesta limited registered balloons first to 750 and now to about 550. Balloons are finding it increasing a problem to find a landing spot because of development.

Balloons kissing. Courtesy of Barbe Awalt

42. Avoid Power Lines at All Costs

We have seen people die when the balloon they are riding in hits power lines. We have also seen them fall as a result of collision with lines. It is no laughing matter. Hats off to PNM (Albuquerque's electric company) for getting crews there to help. We have also seen collisions with radio towers. Avoid PZs—Prohibited Zones. They are airports, usually Native American reservations, military bases, and other places that have requested to be a PZ. Livestock, as a rule, hate to hear or see balloons. It freaks them out. Do not land in a horse field.—www.hotairballooning.org/uploads/crewdev_brochure.pdf

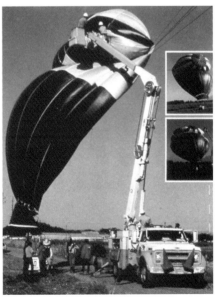

PNM cherry picker pulling balloon out of power lines. Courtesy of Tom McConnell

41. Sponsor a Balloon

When we started doing ballooning many years ago, sponsors got an ad in the Balloon Fiesta program, jackets, special passes to allow you to go in the Sponsor tent; most important, sponsoring a balloon gave one a chance to get to know the pilots and crew of a balloon. We have to say those Sponsor Tents are awfully nice! Did you know they have bathrooms and food?

After Midnight balloon with the sponsor banner for the Albuquerque Public Schools Centennial Program. Courtesy of Barbe Awalt

40. Learn Who Is in the Ballooning Hall of Fame

There are actually three Halls of Fame: The National Balloon Museum, the Ballooning Federation of America, and the Albuquerque International Balloon Fiesta®. These have some of the same people but some are very different. The National Balloon Museum has people like: Malcolm Forbes, Joe Kittinger, and Tom Sheppard. The Balloon Fiesta Hall of Fame has: Mayor Harry Kinney, Kim Vesely, Jodi Baugh, Marge & Bob Ruppenthal, and Dr. Tom McConnell. All three have people like: Carol Rymer Davis, Maxie Anderson, Ben Abruzzo, and Sid Cutter. It is a who's who of ballooning. The International Hall of Fame affiliated with the Ballooning Commission of the Federated Aeronatique Internationale is housed at the Anderson-Abruzzo Albuquerque International Balloon Museum.—www.nationalballoonmuseum. com/HallofFame.aspx; www.balloonfiesta.com/history/ balloon-fiesta-hall-of-fame; www.bfa.net

Ballooning Hall of Fame at National Balloon Museum. Courtesy of National Balloon Museum

39. Remember Balloons & Drones Don't Go Together

Hot air balloons and drones do not work well together. Drones can punch holes in the envelope of balloons causing it to deflate. Balloons can't get out of the way of a drone. Balloons also don't do well with: powerlines, cigarettes, high wind, barbed wire fences, gas tank explosions, or gun shots. Yes, we have seen them all. Hot air balloons are very sturdy but certain things aimed at the envelope put everyone in danger—in the basket and on the ground. In Egypt, a tourist balloon holding 18 people plus the pilot crashed after the tank in the balloon basket exploded. Safety inspections are a very good thing.—www.cnn.com/2013/02/26/world/Africa/balloon-safety-explainer/

Fiesta balloon at Taos Balloon Rally, Courtesy of John T. Denne

38. Daydream You Can Fly

Have you ever looked up in the sky and thought I would like to fly? There are just a few ways you can fly and hot air balloons let you feel, experience, hear, and see the sights of ballooning.

Balloon landing outside of Museum window. Courtesy of Anderson-Abruzzo Albuquerque International Balloon Museum

37. Brazil, the New Powerhouse?

Until recently, special shape balloons came from Europe or the USA. Brazil has become the new power in special shapes. Their balloons include: the Bee Family, FMG for the Gatineau Hot Air Balloon Festival, Jewel the Hummingbird, Pea-Nut The Elephant, and in 2014 Aquario the Fish Bowl. There are many other crowd-pleasing shapes.—http://krqe.com/2014/10/02/brazilina-pilot-returns-to-balloon-fiesta-with-new-special-shape/

Super FMG courtesy of the Gatineau Hot Air Balloon Festival, Canada. FMG is the first balloon in the history of hot air ballooning to be made by two companies: Marcus Bonimcontro of RVB Ballooning (Sao Paolo, Brazil) designed it and Cameron Balloons(Bristol, England) built it.

36. Learn the Parts of a Hot Air Balloon

You just can't call it a red-thingy, or where the flame comes out, or where is the brake? If you are going to be involved in ballooning you need to know the proper names for everything. Also learn that a fire extinguisher needs to be in the basket!—www.planoballoonfest. org/pilots-balloons/anatomy-of-a-hot-air-balloon

Balloon diagram. Courtesy of Paul Rhetts and Rio Grande Books

35. Talk to an Age-Challenged Pilot about the Balloon Parade

It is a different time. You need to talk to an original pilot to learn about the parades, flights, rules or lack of them, and how it was many years ago. The Balloon Fiesta Parade went down Central in Albuquerque on the Saturday of Fiesta. Many of the crews, with hot air balloons, dressed up—even wearing togas! It is fun to hear how ballooning was and how it isn't now. Now we have many more rules!

Pilots Tom McConnell, Frank Bacon, and Bill Douglas in front of the Sun Flyer chase crew vehicle at the 2014 Balloon Fiesta. Courtesy of Paul Rhetts

34. Tag Your Kids

On any given day, over 100,000 people come to a Fiesta event. If you go to any balloon event show your kids where to meet if separated, where the police are headquartered, and where your balloon is located. At Balloon Fiesta in Albuquerque, the police tag kids with IDs just in case.

Kids swarm around a balloon that just landed. Courtesy of Barbe Awalt

33. Try a Balloon Wine, Salsa, or Dog Cookie

The Anderson Valley Vineyards in the North Valley of Albuquerque made great wine. The Vineyard was owned by Maxie Anderson and his wife. They have had balloon themed wines and the Balloon Blush was our favorite. Alas, they aren't in business any more but there are wonderful New Mexico wines to sample. There is also salsa, and Barker's Bakery Balloon Dog Treats. We have other good stuff in New Mexico—not just hot air balloons.

Anderson Valley Vineyards wine bottle label featuring special Balloon Fiesta Blush.

32. Bring Water and Drinks

Hydrate! No matter where you are. Ballooning means you out in a pick-up or in the air. They are all hard work and dehydrating. The crew needs to drink water, juice, or soft drinks. No alcohol please until the balloon is packed up. Always pack a cooler. Speaking of packing the envelope, have you ever lost wedding rings, gloves, hats, purses, or people in the envelope? We have!

Mass Ascension at Balloon Fiesta. Courtesy of Barbe Awalt

31. Bring Phones

Just like you bring drinks, make sure everyone has a cell-phone. The balloon can land in an isolated place and the pilot needs to communicate with the crew. The crew needs to communicate if they are stuck in traffic. Before the cell-phone craze, our balloon landed on the volcanoes in the West Mesa. We needed a phone then! The pilot can see where to land and the access roads to get to the balloon. And after everything is all over, you need to call for reservations to eat. Priorities.

A rough landing on the West Mesa. Courtesy of Barbe Awalt

30. Collect Official Posters

Every year there is an Official Fiesta Balloon Poster. Without question each is wonderful and the early posters are real collector's items. Get a poster, have it framed, and put it up on your wall to remind you about ballooning.—www.balloonfiesta.com

Official Balloon Fiesta poster, 2015. Artist: Victoria de Almeida.

29. See Malcolm Forbes Balloons – AH!

Malcolm Forbes came on our radar in the 1980s and 1990s as Editor of *Forbes Magazine*. He was also a licensed hot air balloon pilot taking up the sport at age 48. Forbes set records including the 1973 first ride across America in a hot air balloon. He also founded in 1973, the first hot air balloon museum in Normandy, France, at Forbes' Château de Balleroy. Forbes was named to the Board of Directors of the Balloon Federation of America in 1974. In 1976 he was elected as Executive Vice President of the National Aeronautic Association. His special shapes, especially for Friendship Tours included: Minar, Santa Maria, Beethoven, Sphinx, the Golden Temple, Château de Balleroy (two of them), the Macaw, and Motorcycle. Forbes was inducted into the National Balloon Museum Hall of Fame.—http://www.nationalballoonmuseum.com/HallofFame.aspx

Malcolm Forbes Hall of Fame plaque. Courtesy of National Balloon Museum

28. Get Engaged or Married in a Balloon

The nicest place to get engaged or married is in a hot air balloon. Usually, there is at least one event every year at Fiesta. You can also do it without thousands of people around by renting your own balloon anywhere. Just be a little flexible with the weather. To get married in a balloon, it helps to have a big balloon—pilot, wedding couple, preacher, and any family or friends. It can be as large or small as you want. Don't forget someone to take pictures in the balloon and on the ground.

Engagement banner. Courtesy Ana & Josh Bacon

27. Take Up VIPS in Your Balloon

Part of the fun of owning a balloon is taking up VIPs for their first ride. We have seen on the news: Governors, movie stars, national political candidates, Broadway actors and crew, and of course local TV personalities. Even the Archbishop of Santa Fe rode in our balloon as did Tibetan Monks. After a VIP takes a ride, shoot lots of pictures! Make sure they land safely first.

Christening Archbishop Michael J. Sheehan after his first flight. Courtesy of Barbe Awalt

26. Make Sure Someone on Your Crew Knows First Aid

From simple cuts and bruises to life threatening injuries, you need someone who can deal with blood. Balloons need first aid kits and fire extinguishers for emergencies. Some balloons even require helmets for passengers. You also need a phone to call for fire, ambulance, or police help. It doesn't hurt to have water and a blanket for that reason. That is a great thing for Chase Crews to have available. We have even had to stop and pull over for a traffic accident and help. Ballooning takes second to emergencies.

Crews all lined up ready to fly. Courtesy of Barbe Awalt

25. Look Up and See Balloons

Not while you are driving! Take some time when you have nothing better to do and look at balloons. After all, if you sit in traffic enjoy the view! Pull over and just watch.

Lots of balloons at Balloon Fiesta. Courtesy of Barbe Awalt

24. Write a Balloon Book

If you are into ballooning, studied it, gathering information over the years, taken a bunch of pictures, you need to share that information. If you have special access you need to share. The early balloonists need to have their stories told before they are no longer with us. We are just realizing that we were blessed with people who made ballooning happen for us to enjoy. It was a different world 20 or 30 years ago. Capture those stories while you can.

Balloon Safety Seminars *book by Dr. Tom McConnell Courtesy of Rio Grande Books, publisher*

23. Know the 13 Original Fiesta Balloonists

The 13 Original Fiesta Balloonists have gone down in history as starting something that is bigger that anyone could have imagined. Know who they were: Don Kersten, Oscar Kratz, Bill Cutter, Sid Cutter, Dennis Floden, Bill Murtorff, Donald Piccard, Gene Dennis, Matt Wiederkehr, Wilma Piccard, Brent Stockwell, Carter Twedt, and Karl Stefan.

The original 13 balloonists in 1972. Courtesy of Tom McConnell and Patrick Murphy

22. Say Hi to a Horse or Two

The Mounted Police from Albuquerque Police Department, New Mexico Mounted Search & Rescue, and Bernalillo County Sheriff's Department are important to keep the spectators and balloons safe. It is very good to take kids to meet the horses but approach slowly and ask permission to touch. Horses attract kids like a magnet. Who doesn't love a horse?—http://nmmsar. org

New Mexico Mounted Search & Rescue Patrol at Balloon Fiesta. Courtesy of Kristy Hannun Baker

21. Go to a Concert on the Fiesta Field

From the Star Spangled Banner bands at day, to big names at night, Fiesta has music. The Anderson-Abruzzo Albuquerque International Balloon Museum also has music for Furry Friends Fiesta. Private parties at night have music right before the fireworks.

Band at Furry Friends Concert at Anderson-Abruzzo Albuquerque International Balloon Museum during Balloon Fiesta. Courtesy of Barbe Awalt

20. What is the Hare & Hound?

The Hare & Hound Competition race is used at many rallies. The Hare balloon takes off and the Hound balloon chases the Hare balloon. The Hare changes altitude to make the race more interesting and more difficult. The score is determined when a balloon throws a marker bag closest to the Hare balloon marker. Variations on the Hare & Hound are a card game or launching off-field and throwing marker bags at targets on the field.

The original balloon competition was called the Coyote-Roadrunner Race and was invented by Sid Cutter in 1972.

Zia Balloon and the World Balloon flying the American flag. Courtesy of Tom McConnell

19. Go to a ABQ Aloft Location

Albuquerque Aloft™ starts off the Fiesta craziness by going to Albuquerque Public Schools and Rio Rancho Public School early on the Friday of the first Fiesta weekend. The event started in 2001 to let the students, teachers, parents, and community get up close and personal with balloons. They could be tethering or launch from the school. KKOB radio coordinates activities that morning. It is the only Fiesta event not attached to flying to or from the field.—www.balloonfiesta.com/event-info/albuquerque-aloft

Albuquerque Aloft at Los Ranchos Elementary School, 2001. Courtesy of Barbe Awalt

18. Think Delayed Response & Propane Levels

When piloting a balloon, you have to get used to thinking ahead—delayed response. You can't stop on a dime. There is an art to anticipation. The newest research, by Frank Bacon of *Sun Flyer*, is about "Lower Propane Pressures In Hot Air Balloons." You may roll your eyes or think this is way too technical to think about, but this is a safety concern for everyone flying. If you fly you need to know why propane pressure may be deceiving as the tank becomes low.—www.sunflyerballoon.com/sunflyer2.html

After Midnight balloon inflation. Courtesy of Barbe Awalt

17. Drive a Really Cool Chase Vehicle

Of course you can have a pick-up truck and trailer but there are so many more options. Trolleys, converted fire trucks, vans converted for the balloon and crew, and school buses can be seen in use for ballooning. As you get older a lift is wonderful. Room for everything is the first priority. A rolling bathroom would be a crew pleaser. Priority is room for coolers.

Sun Flyer Trolley chase vehicle during a Mass Ascension. Courtesy of Barbe Awalt

16. Visit Saga, Japan

Yes, we know you need to spend a lot of money to go to Japan. The Saga International Balloon Fiesta is the largest ballooning event in Asia. The six-day event is at the end of October. The event started small in 1978 in Kyushu, Japan. In 1980, the event moved to Saga, Japan, and changed its name to Saga International Balloon Fiesta. Saga was also the launch of the record setting, Two Eagles gas balloon in 2015. In 2016, Saga will be the site of the 2016 World Balloon Championship. They have hosted the Championships twice before.—www.sibf.jp

Troy Bradley and Leonid Tiukhtyaev are ready to start their record-breaking flight from Japan across the Pacific. Courtesy of Tami Bradley

15. Help Train the Next Generation

Face it—we are getting older. Pilots step down because they can't comfortably fly. Insurance won't cover advancing age. Older crew members can't lift tonnage. But when you have to step down the knowledge of years of flying can still be used. The most important job is to train a new generation to take over. New pilots, new crew, and sharing experiences. Kids in families become adults and they can learn to fly or crew. We need them!

Last minute instructions from Zebra to Dianna Douglas, 2nd generation pilot, who is ready to take flight. Courtesy of Barbe Awalt

14. Visit the National Balloon Museum & Classic

The National Balloon Museum is in Indianola, Iowa. Yes, there is more than one museum for ballooning. The Museum has a structure that suggests two inverted balloons. When you enter it feels like going into an inflated balloon before it is heated enough to stand up. They have exhibits, a Children's Learning Center, theater, a library, and their own Hall of Fame. The Museum is open 7 days a week and is $3 for entrance. Indianola is also the home of the National Balloon Classic in July.—www.nationalballoonmuseum.com, www.nationalballoonclassic.com

Balloon over the museum. Courtesy of National Balloon Museum

13. Dress in Layers

No matter what kind of balloon event you go to, it starts early! It will be colder than mid-afternoon. You can always take off jackets, hats, and gloves but if you don't have anything to put on, you are out of luck. Remember to take a camera, phone, water, munchies, and maybe even a flashlight. We have seen on the Fiesta Field, women wearing high heels—what about this doesn't work?

Balloons inflating at Balloon Fiesta. Courtesy of Barbe Awalt

12. Study the Winds

You do know hot air balloons can't steer—don't you? You ride currents of wind at different altitudes. The winds can change and sometimes when you land the winds has increased to dangerous levels slamming you into a river, barbed wire, or a field. We have even seen landings into a tent or a vehicle—not good! Wind is forecasted by weathermen. The *piball* (helium-filled "pilot balloon"), let go by pilots before launching, shows the wind speed and direction as it gains altitude.

Balloons going in all directions at Balloon Fiesta. Courtesy of Barbe Awalt

11. Build a Relationship with a Balloon Repair Guy or Gal

You know you will need them! Aerco is the company we use and they have gotten us out of the weeds. You will have burns, tears, and burners that don't work. You will need it done yesterday and most repair places do it. Aerco—www.aercoballoonport.com

Aerco balloon repair facility. Courtesy of Barbe Awalt

10. Join the BFA

The Balloon Federation of America of BFA, is dedicated to the sport and science of lighter-than-air aviation, hot air ballooning, and gas ballooning. BFA was founded in 1961 and membership is open to anyone. Each year, BFA holds a convention, sponsors the US Nationals, the Gordon Bennett Race, publishes *Ballooning*—the Journal of BFA, awards, a camp for kids, and much more. The concerns and missions of BFA involve balloon safety, balloon education, fairness in competitions, and contributions to the sport of ballooning.—www.bfa.net

Balloon Federation of America logo.

9. Be a Young Pilot

Bobby Bradley made history as the youngest, solo, hot air balloon pilot at age 9. The flight took place in Tomé, New Mexico in July, 2011. It doesn't hurt that his dad is Troy Bradley of ballooning fame. Bobby flew in Heavenly Dream, a SkyDye balloon.—www.world recordacademy.com

Other young balloonists: Chloe Hallett of Shropshire, England—youngest girl in England at 17 or Milli Karlstom 17 of Northwood Middlesex, Nick Donner—at age 17 was the youngest pilot to win the U.S. National Hot Air Balloon Championship in 2001.

Heavenly Dream, flown by Bobby Bradley, world's youngest balloon pilot. Courtesy of Tania Goldfeder

8. Not All Balloons Go Up

Yes, you can fly down. It was done in 2014 in Mamet Cave in Croatia. The cave was so large that it allowed a real, but smaller, hot air balloon to fly down, all the way down. The adventurer was Austrian pilot, Ivan Trifonov. He traveled underground 206 meters for 25 minutes. He holds four Guinness World Records for hot air ballooning including the first flights over the North and South Poles. Imagine what you could see!—www.theguardian.com/travel/2014/sep/30/worlds-first-underground-hot-air-balloon-flight-completed-in-croatia

Courtesy of Ivan Trifonov

7. Watch Dawn Patrol

Go early to Fiesta or any other event, and watch the few balloons go up in the dark. They have special lights that allow them to fly in the dark. When they add propane the envelope lights up. The Dawn Patrol helps the other balloon learn about wind speeds at different elevations. But they are awe inspiring and the view from above in the dark must be inspiring.—www. balloonfiesta.com

Dawn Patrol at Balloon Fiesta. Courtesy of Kim Vesely

6. Help Design a Balloon Trading Card

The balloon trading cards started as a way to give the crowds something but not give them a pin that is considerably more in cost. The cards are about $17.50 plus shipping for 1,000 whereas pins are about $1@. The cards usually have on the front the balloon and the name of the balloon and on the back is the pilot and balloon facts. They are especially good for schools and not as heavy in your pocket as a bunch of pins.—www. balloonsgalore.us/trading cards.html, www.balloon-cards.net

Freedom Flight POW-MIA Balloon trading card (front). Smokey Bear Balloon trading card (back).

5. Help Design a Balloon Pin

Everyone in the balloon world swarms for the "official" balloon pins for Balloon Fiesta. There are pins for each event, the year of Fiesta, Chase Crew, propane, security, police, and some are sold to further the mounted police. Every group has treasured pins like the zebras, media, weather, TV stations, and even different balloons have their own pins. Pins are a big deal at Fiesta and other ballooning events too! To see a really large group of pins on display, visit the Anderson-Abruzzo Albuquerque International Balloon Museum or attend a pin swap.

Official Albuquerque International Balloon Fiesta® pin for 2004, made up of six separate pins. Courtesy of Tom McConnell

4. Hug a Pilot

Without balloon pilots there would be no ballooning or events. Sometimes that gets lost in all the money changing hands. Every pilot I have known has been true blue, looks out for others, and keeps all the pieces of flying in their heads. Pilots train, learn the rules, and take flying and safety seriously. They can even manage to be awake and welcoming to crew at 4am. If hugs are too much for you, thank a pilot. It isn't said enough.

Balloon Pilot Emeritus Bill Douglas. Courtesy Barbe Awalt

3. Buy a Hot Air Balloon

It is a huge adventure—naming it, designing it, and the first flight. Of course there is the cost but we don't want to even go there. Our last balloon was named in a contest with the local elementary school. The *ohhs* and *ahhs* are worth it. After all, it is only money! There is no feeling like flying.—www.sunflyerballoon.com

Sun Flyer balloon. Courtesy of Barbe Awalt

2. Visit the Anderson-Abruzzo Albuquerque Intn'l Balloon Museum

It was meant to happen. We needed a world-class museum to celebrate ballooning and all the history of balloons we have in New Mexico. So in 2005, it was built. The Museum looks like a hot air balloon inflating. The Anderson-Abruzzo Albuquerque International Balloon Museum has the best view of the Fiesta field. It has permanent and temporary exhibits of all types of ballooning. It even was a command center for the Two Eagles gas balloon flight. There are: Stories in the Sky for kids, special events, meeting spaces for the community, and it serves as a rental for weddings. It also hosts the Balloons & Breakfast and Dine & Glow (formerly Diamond Club) and Furry Friends Fiesta during the Balloon Fiesta. Who could miss the Chic-I-Boom Ball. It also has a fun Shoppe. There is so much to love about the Museum!—www.balloonmuseum.com

Balloons over the museum. Courtesy of Anderson-Abruzzo Albuquerque International Balloon Museum

1. Attend Albuquerque International Balloon Fiesta®

What can we say—this is the greatest show on earth or in the sky. So many people make it work all year, the Fiesta is massive for ten days—night or day. There are products, events, and every person can participate. We say ten days because Albuquerque Aloft™ starts off things. It is just not pilots and chase crews, though without them there wouldn't be Fiesta. Without Fiesta, Albuquerque might not be the "Hot Air Capitol of the World."

Fiesta balloon. Courtesy of John T. Denne

Suggested Websites

www.balloonmuseum.com
www.balloonfiesta.com
www.nationalballoonmuseum.com
www.bfa.net
http://ballongaz.free.fr
www.hotairballooning.org
www.associationmontgolfiere.com
www.sib.jp/e/organization/
www.gasballooning.org

Aerial view of Balloon Fiesta field in 2003. Courtesy of Tom Mc-Connell

Near Misses

We asked people on various social media channels to send in their best Bucket List entries. Here are some of them:

Learn about the Lines of Nazca (see Space Pioneers: In Their Own Words, *pp. 581-583)—Loretta Hall*

Organize a small balloon rally in your home town—Tom McConnell

Show off your status by buying a Pilot's jacket—Paul Rhetts

Get together with a great crew—Barbara Douglas

Learn to weave a wicker balloon basket—Tom McConnell

Put a balloon bumper sticker on your car—Barbe Awalt

Put together all the things you need to be able to fly—Bill Douglas, pilot emeritus

Apply for summer BFA balloon camp—Tom McConnell

Royal Balloons over tent rocks in Cappadocia, Turkey. Courtesy of Chief Pilot Suat Ulusoy

Albuquerque International Balloon Fiesta® Hall of Fame

Hall of Fame inductees have contributed to the success of the Balloon Fiesta through their gifts of time, energy and talent. Past inductees include:

Sid Cutter	Aubrey Cookman
Tom Rutherford	Mark Sullivan
Charles L. Hines	Jodi Baugh
Harry Kinney	Linda Rutherford
Ben Abruzzo	George Hahn
Maxie Anderson	JW Byrd
John C. Davis IV	Frank Mezzancello
Sheri Moore	Carol Rymer Davis
Marge Ruppenthal	Steve Yazzie
Bob Ruppenthal	Al Tetreault
Jacqueline Hockey	Harry T. Season
Jim Shiver	Pat J. Brake
Al Kinney	Bruce King
Thomas McConnell, MD	Sam Baxter
Bruce W. Hale	Richard Abruzzo
Jim "Badtoe" Benson	Ray Bair
Jim Baca	Rodney A. May
Betty Perkins	Kim Vesely

Official Balloon Fiesta bumper sticker, 2014

ALBUQUERQUE INTERNAT

WALL O

Ben Abruzzo
HALL OF FAME 1985

Richard Abruzzo
HALL OF FAME 2011

Maxie Anderson
HALL OF FAME 1985

Scott Appelman
HERITAGE AWARD 2013

Jim Baca
HALL OF FAME 1998

Ray Bair
PRESIDENT 2008-09
HALL OF FAME 2012

Jodi Baugh
HALL OF FAME 1999

J. W. Byrd
HALL OF FAME 2004

Ron Caldwell
BALLOONMEISTER 1980

Aubrey Cookman
HALL OF FAME 1998

Neida Courtney-Bueno
BALLOONMEISTER 2011-12

Sid Cutter
BALLOONMEISTER 1972, 1974-75
EXECUTIVE DIRECTOR 1973-75
HALL OF FAME 1983
HERITAGE AWARD 2011

Carol Rymer Davis
HALL OF FAME 2005

John Davis
BALLOONMEISTER 1968-69
PRESIDENT 1985
HALL OF FAME 1985
HERITAGE AWARD 2006

Charles Hines
PRESIDENT 1977, 1985
HALL OF FAME 1984

Jacqueline Hockey
HALL OF FAME 1992

Bruce King
HALL OF FAME 2010

Gary King
BALLOONMEISTER 2002-03

Al Kinney
HALL OF FAME 1994

Charlotte Kinney
BALLOONMEISTER 1982, 1984

Harry Kinney
HALL OF FAME 1984

Neida Courtney Naumberg
BALLOONMEISTER 1983-84

Sam Parks
BALLOONMEISTER 2013-14

Betty Perkins
PRESIDENT 1975-76
HALL OF FAME 1998

Chuck Raskob
BALLOONMEISTER 2009-10

Allen Rector
BALLOONMEISTER 1998

Dick Rice
PRESIDENT 1983

Mike Rice
PRESIDENT 2014

Jim Shiver
PRESIDENT 1986-88
HALL OF FAME 1993
HERITAGE AWARD 2011

Gail Short
PRESIDENT 1984

Paul Smith
EXECUTIVE DIRECTOR 1997-PRESENT

Mark Sullivan
PRESIDENT 1997-98
HALL OF FAME 1999

Art Swenka
PRESIDENT 2002-03

Sixty-seven members of the Albuquerque International Balloon Fiesta®

108

Sam Baxter
HALL OF FAME 2011

Gary Bennett
PRESIDENT 2006-07

Jim Benson
HALL OF FAME 1995

Wally Book
BALLOONMEISTER 2001-02
HERITAGE AWARD 2014

Pat Brake
BALLOONMEISTER 1996-97
EVENT DIRECTOR 1998-2010

Dick Brown
HERITAGE AWARD 2012

Dick Butterfield
BALLOONMEISTER 1990-91

Don Draper
BALLOONMEISTER 1972

Don Edwards
EVENT DIRECTOR 2010-PRESENT

Paul Enz
BALLOONMEISTER 1981

Doug Gallagher
BALLOONMEISTER 1985

George Hahn
BALLOONMEISTER 1986-87
PRESIDENT 1991
HALL OF FAME 2002

Bruce Hale
PRESIDENT 1995-96
HALL OF FAME 1997

Sam Hancock
EXECUTIVE DIRECTOR 1996

Steve Komadina
PRESIDENT 1999

Cheryl Lete
BALLOONMEISTER 2006-08

Doug March
BALLOONMEISTER 1977-78

Rod May
BALLOONMEISTER 1994-95
PRESIDENT 2000-01
HALL OF FAME 2012

Tom McConnell
PRESIDENT 1992
HALL OF FAME 1995
HERITAGE AWARD 2008

Frank Mezzancello
PRESIDENT 1984
HALL OF FAME 2004

Sheri Moore
PRESIDENT 1978-79
HALL OF FAME 1987

Bob Ruppenthal
BALLOONMEISTER 1976
PRESIDENT 1989-90
HALL OF FAME 1998
HERITAGE AWARD 2007

Marge Ruppenthal
PRESIDENT 1980-81
EXECUTIVE DIRECTOR 1985-95
HALL OF FAME 1988
HERITAGE AWARD 2007

Linda Ratherford
HALL OF FAME 2001

Tom Rutherford
HALL OF FAME 1983
HERITAGE AWARD 2010

Jim Schumacher
PRESIDENT 1993

Harry Season
BALLOONMEISTER 1992-97
PRESIDENT 2000-99
HALL OF FAME 2009

John Sena
PRESIDENT 2010-11
HALL OF FAME 2013

Al Tetreault
HALL OF FAME 2007

Kim Vesely
HERITAGE AWARD 2009
HALL OF FAME 2012

Bill Walker
PRESIDENT 2012-13

Mark Wilson
BALLOONMEISTER 1979

Steve Yazzie
BALLOONMEISTER 1999-2000
HALL OF FAME 2006

Ed Yost
BALLOONMEISTER 1972

Wall of Fame. Courtesy of Tom McConnell and AIBF

Zia Balloon Chainsaw art by Mark Chavez at Balloon Fiesta. Courtesy of Tom McConnell

Build Your Own Bucket List

1.

2.

3.

4.

5.

6.

7.

8.

9.

10.

11.

12.

13.

14.

15.

16.

17.

18.

19.

20.

21.

22.

23.

24.

25.

26.

27.

28.

29.

30.

31.

32.

33.

34.

35.

36.

37.

38.

39.

40.

41.

42.

43.

44.

45.

46.

47.

48.

49.

50.

51.

52.

53.

54.

55.

56.

57.

58.

59.

60.

61.

113

62.

63.

64.

65.

66.

67.

68.

69.

70.

71.

72.

73.

74.

75.

76.

77.

78.

79.

80.

81.

82.

83.

84.

85.

86.

87.

88.

89.

90.

91.

92.

93.

94.

95.

96.

97.

98.

99.

100.

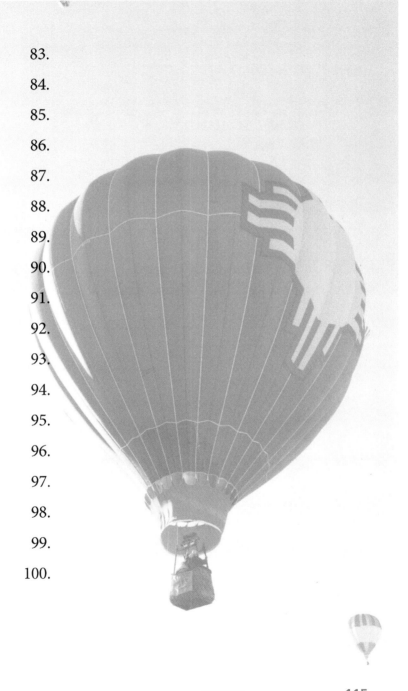

ANDERSON-ABRUZZO ALBUQUERQUE INTERNATIONAL BALLOON MUSEUM FOUNDATION

The Anderson-Abruzzo Albuquerque International Balloon Museum Foundation is a 501(c)(3) non-profit organization established to raise funds, to foster public recognition, and to promote and build membership for the Anderson-Abruzzo Albuquerque International Balloon Museum. The Balloon Museum is a collaborative project of the Foundation and the City of Albuquerque Cultural Services Division. Membership in the Anderson-Abruzzo Albuquerque International Balloon Museum Foundation is your ticket to "high flying" adventures! In addition to year round free Balloon Museum admission, your membership entitles you to fascinating shows and special events in one of the most spectacular settings imaginable. For more information www.balloonmuseum.com

ABOUT THE AUTHOR

Barbe Awalt, an author, publisher, and photographer, is passionate about New Mexico and ballooning. She, and her husband Paul Rhetts, won the Mother Teresa Award from the St. Bernadette's Institute for Sacred Art and the Millie Santillanes Education Award from the New Mexico Hispanic Preservation League, for their work promoting Hispanic New Mexican art. They also received the Joe Leaphorn Award for support of writers from the Hillerman Mystery Writers Conference. They have published some of the best books about New Mexico. She has been part of a balloon Chase Crew for over 20 years.

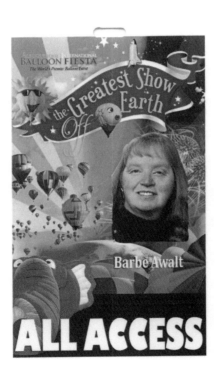

CPSIA information can be obtained at www.ICGtesting.com
Printed in the USA
LVIW01n0007200715
446728LV00001B/1